HISTORY in a HURRY

Ancient Egypt

written and drawn by
JOHN FARMAN

MACMILLAN
CHILDREN'S BOOKS

First published 1997 by Macmillan Children's Books
a division of Macmillan Publishers Limited
25 Eccleston Place, London SW1W 9NF
and Basingstoke

Associated companies throughout the world

ISBN 0 330 35248 2

Text and illustrations copyright © John Farman 1997

The right of John Farman to be identified as the
author of this work has been asserted by him in accordance with the
Copyright, Designs and Patents Act 1988.

3 5 7 9 8 6 4

A CIP catalogue record for this book is available from
the British Library.

Printed and bound by Mackays of Chatham plc, Kent

☁ CONTENTS

OFF WE GO!

What would you say if someone quizzed you on how much you know about Ancient Egypt? If you're anything like me, the result could be tragically short. I usually start with the pyramids and all the slaves it took to build 'em, then I remember those films like *Antony and Cleopatra* or *Carry on Cleo* where all the guys dash round in flash little sports-chariots wearing flash little loincloths and those funny helmets with birds' heads on, while the women stay at home lounging provocatively on gold sofas being fed dusky grapes by duskier slaves. Then I remember those weird 'side-on' paintings where everything looks like it's been run over by a steam roller and all and sundry have two left feet; and then there were mummies; and then . . . and then I usually give up.

Most of my knowledge about the Egyptians is based on cobbled together bits from the aforementioned silly movies (always starring Charlton Heston), or those dreadful all-pictures-with-little-captions books, that simply tell you what you knew already. Now I've researched the subject thoroughly, I know at least twice as much.

My book (all-writing-and-little-pictures) will have a jolly good shot at answering most of the questions that you'd ask if you ever got the chance by covering the whole damn lot as fast as possible.

If you notice annoying scribbles by someone called Ed in this book, I'm sorry, but it's Susie, my fussy editor*. The daft printer left them in by mistake and we didn't have time to change things before printing the book.

*Just doing my job! Ed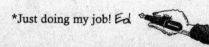

EGYPT: WHERE WAS IT
☼—**AND WHERE IS IT NOW?**[*]

Geographical Bit

To save me drawing a map, get hold of a globe and spin it round till you get to the side with Saudi Arabia facing you. You'll see that the area that we now call Egypt is a rectangle, with Libya on the left, the Red Sea on the right and the Sudan at the bottom. In olden days countries were defined by the sort of people that lived there, rather than by lines drawn on a map (or on the ground). The main difference between then and now, as far as I can see, seems to be that where Egypt and the Sudan join, there used to be a vast country called Nubia (where all the Nubians came from).

Historical Bit

When referring to the great Ancient Egyptian civilization experts usually think of the period between 3200 and 341 BC; by which time all the great things that they have become famous for (and what this book's going to be about) were up and running. But all that famous stuff, Pharaohs, pyramids, etc, didn't come along for thousands of years *after* the first Egyptian-lings settled on the fertile part of this huge land of sand.

[*]Much the same place as it always was, surely? Ed

Just to put you in the picture I'll give a lightning rundown of how the whole business came about from start to finish*. After all, a book on Ancient Egypt wouldn't be the same without one.

6000–3200 BC
Neolithic and Pre-Dynastic Periods
Lots of different cultures involved; only thing worth noting is that it ended with the happy marriage between Upper and Lower Egypt.

3200–2700 BC
Dynasties (lines of family-linked kings) 1–2
Thinite, Early Dynastic and Archaic Periods

Ancient Egypt as we know it starts here. First capital of Egypt was called *This*. Second was probably called *That*, but was later changed to *Memphis*. Egyptians learned how to write hieroglyphically, build buildings using bricks and wood, and construct the first Royal tombs at Abydos.

2700–2300 BC
Dynasties 3–6
The Old Kingdom
Decided to build pyramids, then Sun Temples. Great kings include Zoser, Snofru, Cheops, Chephren and Myceninus.

EARLY BUILDERS' BUMS

*Surely not the WHOLE business. Ed

2300– 2050 BC

Dynasties 7–12

First Intermediate Period

Capitals: Herakeopolis and Thebes. Jolly nasty time for all concerned. Mass chaos, fighting, starvation: general rowdiness. To cap all that there's a Bedouin invasion from the desert. The War Lords of Thebes gradually get the upper hand.

2050–1775 BC

Dynasties 11–12

Middle Kingdom

The capital's still Thebes, but this time they have a few sensible and clever rulers: Mentuhetep I, Amenemhat I, Sesoristis I and II. Best of all the kingdom pushes up (or down) into Nubia and Asia. Lots of good booklearning and craftwork involved.

1775–1575 BC

Dynasties 13–17

Second Intermediate Period

All good things come to an end. The whole Middle Kingdom collapses. Egypt overrun by nomadic chieftains. Chariots invented (then wheels) (then horses).

THAT'S NOT QUITE WHAT I MEANT

1575–1085 BC

Dynasties 18–20

New Kingdoms

Egypt becomes a proper grown-up empire (called . . . The Empire). A time for fab kings and queens: Ahmosis, Tuthmosis I, Hypnosis*, Hatshepsut,

**Don't be silly. Ed

8

Tuthmosis II, Amenophis II, Akhenaton, Horemhab, Rameses I and II. Time for the Valley of the Kings and good old (or young) Tutankhamun and his famous tomb.

1085–330 BC
Dynasties 21–30
Late Dynastic Period

The going starts to get tough. Egypt falls under the control of the Libyans, Ethiopians, Assyrians and Persians (one at a time, of course).

> *. . . end of Ancient Egypt as we know it . . .*

330 BC–AD 342
Greek and Roman Period

Greeks and Romans come in and sweep them *all* away.

AD 641

It all goes horribly wrong for the Romans when the Arabs take all their toys away.

AD 641– *present*

Nothing much to report, except perhaps the building of the Suez Canal joining the Red Sea to the Mediterranean. It was started by Necho II (610–595 BC) and was opened, over 2000 years later, in 1869. (Sounds like the same builders who did my bathroom.)

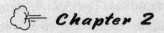

Chapter 2

UPPER AND LOWER, VALLEY AND DELTA

Geographical Bit (again)

You might have noticed (or you might not), a reference, right at the beginning of the last chapter, to Upper and Lower Egypt. To understand how they divide, it's rather important to recognize that the clue is in the River Nile – which runs through both of 'em.

The Nile

The main river Nile is really two rivers in one. The White Nile, which leaks out of Lake Victoria, and the Blue Nile, which trickles down from the lofty mountains of Ethiopia. They join forces at a place which is now called Khartoum, way up in the Sudan. This big new Nile then splits the North African Desert neatly into two. The Western Desert runs towards Libya and the Sahara, and on the other side the Eastern Desert is interrupted by a huge range of mountains before it sweeps down to the Red Sea coastline. Is this getting boring?

The River What?

The very ancient Egyptians didn't actually call the Nile 'The Nile', they called it 'The River'. Pretty logical, for as far as they knew, there weren't any others. They did, however, refer to the lovely slushy green lands round the river, rather oddly, as Kemet – 'the black land'* – and the rest, more appropriately (if rather badly spelt, since it was only desert anyway) as Deshret – 'the red land'.

In really ancient times (pre-Egyptians) the River Nile broke up into lots of junior rivers and streams, which fanned out like . . . a fan, before reaching the sea. This formed an upside-down triangle (map-wise), which became known as the Nile Delta or, in those days, Lower Egypt, with modern Cairo at the bottom or, if you turn the globe the other way up – the top (if you see what I mean). The land surrounding the rest of the Nile going right down (or up in this case) to the mountains, was called Upper Egypt.

The Various Kingdoms

To make things nice and simple (like me) we'll call these two bits where most people lived, the Valley (Upper) and the Delta (Lower). Where they met was the ancient town of Kheraha (just south of modern Cairo).

Further down the river lay the ancient city of Memphis (previously *That*?) which became the King's home and the capital of what has been labelled the 'Old Kingdom'.

The centre of operations for the later 'Middle Kingdom' which came . . . er . . . in the middle, was a little further down-river at the ridiculously spelt Itjtaway (pronounced Itjt-away)**. This general area became the centre for ruling Egypt throughout the 'New Kingdom' and the later, late period (called the 'Late Period').

---

*The black refers to the soil, silly. Ed
** You really are losing it. Ed

Water to Spare

Every year for a hundred days the clouds burst and the rain simply pi . . . poured onto the high lands, causing the main Nile further down (or up)* to burst its banks, flooding the surrounding land and dumping a layer of fine, fertile silt (dirt to you) which had come all the way from Abyssinia.

The early and none too worldly Egyptians were gobsmacked on a yearly basis, not understanding where this extra water came from, but thinking it probably sprang from the underground caves in the Aswan Cataract. Being deeply religious, they interpreted it as a miracle from the guardian of the caves, the good god Khnum (which, of course, it wasn't).

*Don't start all that again. Ed

History (again)

What were the first settlers like? Well, the villagers that hung around the valley of the Nile during the early days became pretty smart. Fed up with all that hunting and gathering, they'd settled down (as settlers do) to a self-sufficient lifestyle, blissfully unaware of what was going on in the rest of the world (which wasn't that much).

They were great stay-at-homers (an Ancient Egyptian travel agent would soon have been out of business): they knew how to grow barley and how to store it; they could run up their own clothes (loin-cloths and stuff), cook decent food and bake bread. They hunted with bows and arrows, kept cattle, goats, sheep and pigs and even invented the dog, cat and goose which they either ate (the geese, that is), or kept as pets.

Let's Get Together

By 4000 BC they were all getting along so well that the different tribes in the Valley (or Upper Egypt) started to think about getting together with the others in the Delta (or Lower Egypt) to form one big country.

Water Talks

Those Valley-people weren't daft. Water has a habit of running downhill, which meant that they could control the river from its source, thus forcing the poor, easy-going Lower Egyptians (living in the Delta) to do as they said by merely threatening to turn off the tap. As you can imagine, this was quite a heavy number, for if the Uppers could take away the Nile, the poor Lowers wouldn't be left with much more than damp sand – and rather a lot of it.

This power that the Uppers had over the Lowers was to dictate the whole course of history in Ancient Egypt. Despite the differences, however, they were quite a relaxed, fun-loving bunch who indulged in none of the dreadful punch-ups and savagery that many other civilizations had to put up with.

Intermediate Strife

But you can't expect any major civilization to keep going for 3000 years without some amount of trouble. There were two great periods of hard times in Egypt. These divided the Old from the Middle Kingdom and the Middle from the New and were called the Intermediate Periods.

They weren't a barrel of laughs if you had to live through them, but they didn't really affect the way that the Egyptians carried on their everyday lives.

The Desert Folk

The poor people that lived in the desert had a much tougher time than the people who lived by the river, having no roads or motorways or boats for that matter*. As it was such an inhospitable sandy land, they preferred to keep on the move the whole time and were therefore what we call 'nomads' (people of no fixed abode).

*Could that be on account of the lack of water? Ed

Pre-Camel Days

They either had to walk to wherever they wanted to go or use the humble donkey for short journeys (or for very long journeys, come to that).

These days we always think of desert people perched on top of camels, but there are no early records of this strange beast. It didn't appear until fairly late in Ancient Egypt's long history, when it became known as the 'ship of the desert' because it could (and still can) cross vast areas of sand without as much as a wet flannel to suck on.

These guys weren't just nomads for the sake of being restless. While travelling from one water hole to another, they traded in spices, animals, ornaments, semi-precious stones, monuments and sand-wiches (not really). Luckily they never stayed put long enough to be any threat to the Valley folk, and largely kept themselves to themselves.

Chapter 3

GOOD THINGS
ABOUT RIVERS

The best thing about rivers is that you can make things float on them. In a land that was only just thinking of the wheel, this became most useful for getting around. As Egyptian river valley people only talked to other Egyptian river valley people they only really needed to go up or down stream (north or south). So, instead of trudging through the boggy reed banks for miles to see their aunties or grannies for tea*, they could hop in their various craft and either sail or paddle up or down stream. They didn't even bother with bridges, tending to go in for ferries (I suppose there was no point if you've got nothing to wheel across them).

Glorious Mud

The other best thing about rivers is that they have a habit of having tons of mud on their bottoms. When you don't have access to a lot of wood, stone, concrete (or prefabricated plastic panels), mud can very useful for building 'mud-castles' to live in, which is just what the ancient Egyptians did.

*Actually, their aunties and grannies would probably have all lived in the same house, so there'd be no need to paddle anywhere. Ed

Early Reeders

The other, other best thing about rivers and the muddy areas that surround them are reeds, and Egypt sure had its fair share. They grew along the banks of the river and throughout the Lower Egyptian Delta. Everywhere you looked you saw reeds, reeds – and then more reeds. Reed on.

There were two types. The first was called the *shema*, and they grew in the Nile Valley in Upper Egypt. For want of something better to name this area, they decided on *ta-shema* which meant – three guesses – 'the land of the shema reed'. The other reed was the *papyrus* and that grew in the Delta. The new name for this land became *ta mehu*, meaning – you're right – 'the land of the papyrus plant'. Reeds were used for loads of things, particularly the papyrus: using the hard outer fibres they made ropes, mats, boxes and sandals, while the soft inside of the stem was used to make the first primitive paper (*The Sun*?).

Chapter 4

SITTING PRETTY
IN THE CITY

OK, that should have set the scene. Now for Ancient Egypt proper. Everything from now on was between 3200 and 341 BC. Seems like a lot to cover but you can't hang around when you're in as much of a hurry as I am.

Studying Egyptian archaeology (old buildings and remains) has its downside. The trouble with making houses out of baked mud, as they did, is that the Egyptian climate (lots and lots of sun followed by lots and lots of rain) has a habit of returning said buildings to their natural state – mud – and who wants to study that?

If that wasn't bad enough Egyptologists (as they call themselves) have to suffer the results of the work of the *sebakheen*. These were peasants who, like human termites, would grovel about looking for *sebakh*, the decomposed mud and straw bricks used to make ancient buildings. They carelessly chucked the *sebakh*, and therefore future generations' history, onto their fields as fertilizer (still, I suppose it beats donkey poo).

New Buildings for Old

This situation was made worse by following generations' annoying habit of pulling down old buildings and using the bits to make new ones; like tearing down St Paul's Cathedral to put up a shopping centre. Logical, but not if you want to leave any records for generations to come.

Monkey Business

But what really caused historians to wake up screaming was the damage that had been done to most of the works of art that weren't safely buried underground.

The blame can be laid squarely at the feet of those dratted early Christian Coptic monks. Hating any imagery that wasn't to do with their own god (God), they got their kicks by travelling around, hammer and chisel at the ready, hacking off the heads and limbs (and not just arms and legs, either!) of the statues, and scrawling rude words on the Pharaoh's inscriptions.

Bright and Beautiful

Because all the remaining buildings and relics we see these days look knackered, one is tempted to think that ancient towns like Memphis and Thebes must have always looked a trifle clapped-out too. No way. When they were new (around 3000 BC) or even quite new, they must have appeared positively sleek – just like the new bits of our cities: important buildings and pyramids were faced with sparkly white limestone.

Who Lived Where?

So what were these towns and cities like?

In the middle were all the religious and government buildings – lots of obelisks, mosques and pinnacles (like Bradford or Wolverhampton). Temples didn't just do religious business like they do these days, but were the central meeting place, and even the trading centre of the city.

Surrounding them were the leafy suburbs of the rich and important, with fab houses, gardens and avenues.

The rest of the teeming population lived in all the spaces in between (as teeming populations have a tendency to do) attaching their shacks and tents to the walls of the main buildings as close to the top palace or temple as possible, mainly because that was where everything happened. Every now and again the Pharaoh of the day, usually in an attempt to tidy up some city or other, would chuck them all out. Gradually, however, and with good reason, they'd sneak back in. You see, the gates to the city would normally be left open at night. But if word came of some approaching horrid horde, waving spears and other miscellaneous sharp things, the doors would be slammed shut – regardless of who was in or out.

Law and Order

For an early civilization, the Egyptians had law and order pretty well sussed. They had proper policemen, tracker-dogs – and tracker-monkeys!* There were courts in every major town and anyone could have their grumble heard.

Most cases were heard by local magistrates and even juries, but the real biggies went in front of the king's Vizier (head of the civil service) in the capital city. If anyone was found to be telling porkies he or she would be treated in a most unpleasant manner. But that was nothing compared to being found guilty of an actual crime.

Petty Crime

For little misdemeanours you could expect a severe ticking off (fists and feet involved) by those Nubian coppers. For crimes like forgery or stealing you'd be lucky not to lose some minor appendage – hand, foot, nose or worse (ouch!!). For treachery you could say goodbye to your tongue, which was about the last thing you would say (apart from 'Aaarrgh!'), and it was the done thing, if found guilty of treason, to top yourself by your own chosen method (thanks for nothing, mate!). If criminals were rich or influential, you'll be amazed (I don't think) to hear that they could usually slip the judge a little something to make him forget (some things never change).

* Are you joking? Ed   No! JF

Chapter 5

HOUSES . . .
⟨≋ EGYPTIAN STYLE

Perhaps the Egyptians' greatest invention ever, and one that we take completely for granted, was the ordinary, bog-standard, no-nonsense household brick, which came either sun-dried or kiln-baked. To help the walls stand up they used reed matting and thin sticks to bind them together. If they couldn't get materials from the Nile . . . they simply couldn't get them, full stop: reeds, mud, plaster, or the rock-hard mineral called gypsum which they made floors out of – all these came from the river.

Tree Free
Egyptian houses hardly used any wood, not because they didn't want to, but because there weren't any woods. Most of the precious trees that were used had been floated down river from the forests upstream. If a rich man decided to move, therefore, he'd take the wife, kids, pets, slaves – and any wooden columns or panels with him (which would really annoy me if I'd just bought his place).

Posh Pads
The houses of the rich and successful were fab. As the king and the high priest of the day set the fashion for most things, their houses were often copied. Just to show off, rich people would

create pocket-sized versions of magnificent temples and palaces. None of your three-up, two-down semis for those boys. It's difficult to say exactly what these houses looked like from the outside, as, for the reasons stated earlier (pay attention at the back!), they didn't tend to last that long – in terms of history.

THIS, FANSHAW, IS A TYPICAL MERCHANT'S HOUSE

... Let's Go In
The best Egyptian houses looked strangely twentieth-century – all straight lines and little fussy ornamentation. The first thing you'd see, if the guards or gardeners let you through the large wooden doors, would be a fab garden with a square pool (they didn't go in for 'round' very much). There would be beautiful palms and bushes full of beautiful birds, beautiful plants with beautiful butterflies flitting about, (and usually a few beautiful bimb– er – hand-maidens flitting about too). All very beautiful. The rich Egyptians certainly knew how to live.

Windows and Stairs
The main difference from today is that they didn't go in for windows much, having just a few square holes in the living areas, usually with bars or grilles. Large windows, in a country where the midday sun could burn your beard off*, and where glass hadn't been invented, would be somewhat surplus to

* We do have female readers, you know. Ed

requirements and a bit daft if all you've got for air-conditioning is some small slave waving a large fan. They didn't go in for stairs much either, so most of the buildings were single storey (apart from pyramids, that were *all* stairs when you come to think of it).

Another big difference was size. The average abode of your top-of-the-range Egyptian would have twenty to thirty fair-sized rooms (just like home – I don't think).

An Evening In

Most grand houses would have a largish, squarish living room where the owner and his wife, kids, cats, budgies and guests would laze around on rugs and cushions* (they weren't that big on furniture). There would be various jugs and pots around containing water for the washing of hands before eating. This was quite necessary as lavs as such were still a little primitive: they had no toilet paper, and those early Egyptians didn't go in for knives and forks much. Draw your own conclusions.

There would also be a handy shrine tucked away somewhere for a little light god-worship when the fancy took them. Winters can get a bit chilly up Egypt way, so there'd be a small brazier (32B?) to burn anything from donkey dung to disobedient slaves.

Bedtime

The most interesting thing about the bedrooms was that they had no beds, just reed mattresses on the floor with a wooden headrest at one end. But they did have bathrooms, being the very first people to think of pipes and plumbing (if only to run the water *away*). There'd usually be a built-in stone

*Not only were budgies not around, but if they were, they certainly wouldn't be 'lazing' around. Ed

slab in the middle where the master and mistress (or should that be mistresses?) could be hosed down and massaged by the built-in slaves.

DID YOU TURN ON THE WATER-MAID? –

Ordinary People's Houses

Most of this book seems to be about the better-off. They're usually the ones that get remembered – that's life. But they were only a very small proportion of the population. The rest lived in much more modest conditions.

OH NO! NOT PREGNANT AGAIN. I'D BETTER START BUILDING

In the big cities your average working man and his average working family lived in an average terraced house that looked as if it'd been built by someone who'd lost the plans but carried on anyway.

They'd start off with the ground floor and, when the family grew, and as the only way to go was up they would simply add more storeys, always using the roof as a makeshift sitting room for those hot summer nights.

They would divide the house into three main areas: private rooms for mum and the kids, doubling as bed- (or mattress-) rooms; an area for dad, who thought himself above anyone else (nothing's changed there!) to entertain his guests in; and an area where they did all the chores, like preparing food, drink and stuff like that.

Poor People's Houses

The above were the ones in the middle – like our middle class. Unfortunately, the rest lived wherever they could – in shacks and tents, on top of shops and generally anywhere there was a space with no one else in it.

Dead People's Houses

The Egyptians had this wacky habit of building nice homes to live in *after* they'd stopped breathing, with plenty of grub to last them (which it most certainly did) in the afterlife and all the necessary mod cons. This certainly beats the grim cremation furnaces or the damp, wooden boxes that we put each other in these days.

The reason that dead people's houses have survived better than live ones', is that they built 'em underground. It was then just a question, thousands of years later, of first finding and then digging out the pesky things.

 *Chapter 6*

WHAT'S FOR TEA,  MUMMY?

In this country we eat so much junk that, eventually, we'll all turn into huge, bloated E numbers. In Ancient Egypt, it was all very different. Obviously in the desert the grub wasn't that good (unless you *like* sand in your sandwiches*) but in the fertile part even the poorest of peasants had a reasonable and well-balanced diet – not a hamburger or tooth-torturing sugary drink to be had for love nor money (which they didn't have anyway). Sugar, you see, hadn't been invented, so nasty things like obesity and tooth rot were almost unheard of.

They did lose their teeth in other ways, however, mostly because the bread, their staple diet, was so rough and gritty (with grit) that it soon wore the old choppers down to stumps.

Lunch is Served
The main meal of the day for rich and poor alike was at lunchtime. The peasants would eat mountains of bread (the sort you could injure your enemies with), a few vegetables like onions, lettuces, radishes or sweetcorn from the backyard, and fish – shoals and shoals of fish (unless you were a follower of

*That's the second time you've used that joke. *Ed*

the nasty god Seth – who seth you shouldn't eat fish). There might be the odd animal or bird for a treat, but that was usually kept for celebrations. Killing your sheep, cow, goat or chicken would be a bit like murdering the milkman, as they were their main source of milk, cheese and eggs when the supermarket was closed*.

Likewise the family pig (and its personal snout) was often used to turn over the ground, as well as to pull things. Making him into bacon would have been a bit of a short-term thrill.

HEADS OR TAILS
PORK OR PORKY?

Mine's a Pint

The main drink was, believe it or not, *beer*, for adults and kids (not fair – I hear you cry) which Dad made in vast quantities. Not the clear, foamy liquid we get today, but soupy, flat, sweet and lumpy (sounds like the stuff they serve in The Dog and Dungheap – my local).

*I thought this was supposed to be a serious book. Ed

Recipe: Real Egyptian Home Brew

 1. Take one big
Ali Baba style pot.

2. Fill with water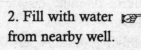
from nearby well.

3. Chuck in a couple of
lightly baked wheat loaves.

4. Add a handful
of barley.

5. Leave for a couple
of months.

6. Strain through an
old sock.

 7. Taste

8. Throw away and
go down the pub
for a pint of
mass-produced lager.

Suppers with the Uppers

The rich Egyptians went short of nothing and probably ate much better than your average Egyptian does now (naff international-style buffets so I've heard). Their gardens were full of fruit trees and they had plenty of peaches, pears, figs, dates, oranges, lemons . . . you name it. Also, in every garden, there would be grape vines curling up Poles* or running up the sides of the buildings. The Egyptians became real experts at the old wine-making.

Salads would be sprinkled with oil from the Bak tree (from out the back), vinegar and salt. They were still waiting for olive oil which arrived with the Greeks (Popeye arrived with the Americans). Luckily castor oil was only used for lighting lamps rather than for pouring down kids' throats to facilitate lavatorial pursuits.

Unlike the poor peasants, eating loads of meat was a huge status symbol for the well-to-do. Nothing was safe – from oxen to gazelles, sheep to oryxs (kind of big deer), pigeons to cranes (kind of big bird).

Pharaoh Phare

As for the Pharaoh, when he sat down for a little light lunch or tea he too could do slightly better than fish fingers and alphabetti spaghetti. On a normal night he could expect many different kinds of bread, several types of meat, a few birds (some to eat and some to watch dancing), fruit salad (unfortunately without ice cream), lots of cakes and two or three kinds of wine.

For feasts and special occasions, he'd have something a little more substantial, of course.

*Shouldn't that be a small p? Ed

Downsides of Eating Egyptian Style

△ Guests might have scented cones of fat put on their heads, designed to melt: smothering the wearer with oil.

△ Beer was sometimes flavoured with prune juice – yukk!

△ Poor people would often have to eat over 2 kilos of gritty bread per day*.

△ The best bit of an animal to eat was . . . its head.

△ Much of the meat they ate was 'jerked' – dried in the sun, then salted.

△ Egyptians were real big on locusts smothered in honey for afters.

I think I'll stick to the Happy Eater.

* So would you if there was nothing else. Ed

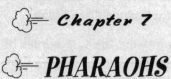

Chapter 7

PHARAOHS

Before checking out how the Pharaoh fared in Ancient Egypt, let's look at the social structure beneath him.

Who Was Who?

△ Directly below the Pharaoh came his right (and left) hand man – the top dog in the civil service – known as the king's Vizier. He took command of the army, squeezed taxes out of the common folk, dished out the law and generally did all the stuff his boss couldn't be bothered to do.

△ After the Vizier came the *imakhu*. These were all the friends, family (and hangers-on) of the Pharaoh. They were given the very best jobs and made sure the Pharaoh didn't have to talk to anyone he didn't want to. (Couldn't we all do with someone like that?)

△ All round Egypt were the regional nobility called the *nomarchs*. They got well above themselves, acting like mini Pharaohs.

△ Next came the scribes, who scribbled everything about everything down. We can thank them for all we now know. Below them were the priests, who did all the talking for the gods. Priests were two-a-penny* in Ancient Egypt.

△ Underneath them were all the craftspeople, who fashioned

*I thought you said they didn't have money. Ed

all the beautiful artefacts that the robbers didn't get their hands on and that we can still see today.

⚠ At the very bottom were the vast hordes of peasants who did what they were told and knew their place. That's what peasants are for, isn't it?

Why Pharaohs?

Various other civilizations had risen and fallen in various other river valleys in the Near East. The trouble was that most of them were simply a haphazard heap of rival city states. By continually scrapping with each other, like any village church committee, they never really got anywhere.

Egypt was different. Very early on the Egyptians discovered that having one top, not-to-be-messed-with, do-as-I-say-or-else, all-powerful king was the best way to go about things. A bit like a kindly dictatorship.

Who Got What?

The land was owned by the crown, a few big landowners and the temples, but everyone right down to the farmers had to pay the Pharaoh taxes: grain, cereal, beer and wine. This made the Pharaoh unbelievably rich (and the farmers unbelievably poor). If crops failed and they couldn't shell out, the farmers would be whipped (I'm surprised our Inland Revenue haven't picked up on this idea).

To your everyday Egyptian, the Pharaoh was actually a god as well and could do no wrong. Lets face it, there's no point being a god/king if you can't do exactly as you jolly well please. I suppose this seems a bit odd when you think of the poor, under-privileged, can't-make-a-decision-about-anything royals *we* have to put up with, but a) the Egyptians actually liked thinking that their kings were perfect and b) there was no gutter press hounding them and snooping on all their after-dark activities.

Top Job
As jobs went, Pharaohing couldn't really have been bettered. If everyone really wants to believe you're the cleverest, strongest, most perfect person in the land, then it's a bit churlish not to let 'em. Duties involved anything from a little light (or should I say heavy) rain-making once a year to flood the Nile; leading armies into battle (making sure nobody actually kills *you*); and looking after (nudge, nudge, wink, wink) loads of wives and concubines.

Switching On

The Pharaoh's main function, however, was to start each day off. Every morning an alarm-slave would wake him up before sunrise; then he'd be washed with a special stuff to restore 'the vital force that flowed therefrom upon the Two Lands' (sounds like a soap ad). He'd then be oiled-up (anointed) and dressed in various smart clobber (crown included) by priests who'd all come dressed as head-god Horus (with bird-head masks on).

Having checked his watch*, he'd then go off to the temple in his four-slave-drive chair and just before the sun peaked over the pyramid, he'd say a few carefully chosen magic words. Hey Presto, there would be light and all the silly Egyptians would go home happy, thinking the boss had done it. Eat your heart out, Paul Daniels!

Two for the Price of One

To get over the problem of the great divide – Upper and Lower Egypt – each Pharaoh contained the two rival forces within his own body, which I'd have thought might have kept him awake at night. These two forces were represented by two gods, Horus from the Lower team, and Seth from the Upper one.

By the fourth dynasty the king was regarded as the descendant of the sun god Re, who, having once ruled Egypt in his own right, got a bit bored and high-tailed it back to his heavens leaving successive kings in charge.

*I've warned you about silliness. Ed

Bad Times for Pharaohs

During the first Intermediate Period, the Pharaoh took a bit of
a knocking when, due to heavy droughts in the Nile Basin, the
people turned on their good king-cum-god and blamed him. A
trifle unfair? Not when you consider that for thousands of
years the Pharaohs had taken the credit for all the good times.

Egypt for Grabs

By the time Amenophis III came along, the Pharaoh had
become the most powerful, un-arguable-with, top-dog ever.
The job just simply couldn't get any better. But when you're at
the very top, there's only way to go – that's down . . .*

By the Late Period, Egypt was simply a tract of land that a
whole bunch of foreigners fought over, be they Persians,
Greeks, Libyans or Kushites. The Egyptians themselves even
went off the idea of their boss being a half-god and turned to
the rather bizarre habit of worshipping animals, which I'd have
thought a touch insulting if I'd been a Pharaoh.

Phunny Phings about Pharaohs

⚠ If ever the Pharaoh's shadow fell on you, you might as well
top yourself. It was the worst curse going.

⚠ If you ever got to kiss his foot, it was really good luck.

⚠ If, however, you only kissed the dust on said foot, you'd
better start saying your prayers!

⚠ Pharaohs were dead sensitive about people using their real
names (which were ever so secret). If you called them
anything but Pharaoh (which meant Great House or Palace)

*You should know! Ed

it was extremely bad news (I reckon we should call our queen 'Buck House' for a laugh).

⚠ Pharaohs had one Great Chief Wife (usually the strongest and bossiest) then a load of cousin-wives, sister-wives and even daughter-wives. Yes, you read it right, they often married their own sisters or kids (urggh! Imagine marrying your sister, boys) and even had more kids with them (disgraceful)! The last group of wives was made up of any of the servant or slave babes that had caught his eye. Marrying your daughters and sisters was encouraged to stop other families getting in on the royalty act.

⚠ His two crowns, red and white, were regarded as goddesses themselves and he even *sat* on the lady god, Isis, who, far from objecting, doubled as a throne.

Downsides to Being a Pharaoh

⚠ Pharaohs were put through rigorous physical tests to prove they were superhuman. They often had to cheat.

⚠ Pharaohs had to get up in the dark every single morning. Otherwise the day wouldn't start and it would be their fault.

⚠ Women could be kings (occasionally) but not queens, which involved a certain amount of cross-dressing (false beards and stuff). Highly babish Cleopatra came much later – but was Greek, so didn't really count.

⚠ Being a god could be lonesome at times, as you were far too fabulous, wise and good for anyone else to talk to (I know the feeling).*

*And just who d'you think you're kidding? Ed

⚠ There was a set time for everything you did. Holding audiences, eating meals, giving judgements, going to the loo, having a bath, taking a walk, or even sleeping with the wives. Boring or what?

⚠ Because of all the dodgy interbreeding, the Pharaohs were often a bit dippy and sometimes barking mad.

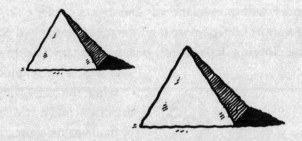

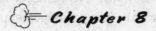

Chapter 8

LOOKING GOOD IN PHARAOHLAND

If you study the frescoes in the palaces, tombs and temples, you'll notice that the average Egyptian was broad-shouldered and slender, with muscular arms and legs, a square chin, wide lips and a short hooked nose (and the men weren't bad either).

In the clothing department, peasants usually had to make do with a lowly loincloth, while the rich – surprise, surprise – had a wide range of made-to-measure, haute-couture clothing. It was not unknown for servants, slaves and kids to run around as bare as the day they were born, since a) Egyptians didn't have a problem with nudity, and b) it was generally nice and warm.

You're not going out dressed like that – are you?

Clothes Shopping Egyptian-Style

Actually, to be totally truthful*, there were no clothes stores in ancient Egypt. Clothes were run-up to order by skilled dressmakers and tailors. The main robe (always sparkly white)

*That makes a change. Ed

worn by the guys was nothing to write home about, but by the time he'd smothered it with sashes and belts, and put on all his necklaces, bracelets and a little make-up he looked rather fab (if a trifle poncy).

Women's robes were more fancy, still white and sari-ish, but covered in pleats, straps, beads and embroidery. If they used any colour at all, it would probably be purple, the dye of which was obtained from the Mediterranean whelk (without his permission) or red, from a herbaceous plant known as the madder family (which made them even madder).

Fit for a King
Strangely enough, the Pharaohs, especially from the Old Kingdom, were really quite restrained when it came to everyday wear. They favoured a mini-skirt, usually embroidered in gold, but nothing much from the waist up (or knee down). Later, in the days of the New Kingdom, they'd just don a simple robe. They never went out, however, without a socking great crown (either white or red) and some dead flash jewellry just to let everyone know who they were. On special days they'd wear a special double crown which combined both white and red (representing Upper and Lower Egypt) but looked a bit prattish as it tended to be a little on the top-heavy side.

On extra-special days they'd wear the extra-special *atef* crown, which was so over-the-top and heavy that the poor chap underneath could barely walk straight. It was covered in long feathers, ram's horns and sacred curly snakes (sounds like something you might see at Ascot). The whole confection was smothered in little shiny discs to represent the sun.

Hair Today, Gone Yesterday

Unlike modern Egyptians, the ancients were quite hairless*. The Pharaoh, therefore, would often wear a stick-on beard, attached to his stuck-on crown (to make himself look tough) and, just to complete the ensemble, he'd put on a fancy wig, which he'd keep beside the bed.

The Downside of Dressing Egyptian

⚠ False beards look stupid.

⚠ Wigs look soppy.

⚠ Women had holes the size of tennis balls in their ears to accommodate all the jewellry.

⚠ Most peasants didn't own a pair of shoes in their whole lives.

*All over?! Ed

 *Chapter 9*

DEAD LUCKY . . .
HOW TO KEEP YOUR
MUMMY COOL

What would you do if your soul's heavenly happiness depended on your earthly (but dead) body remaining in tip-top nick? Tricky, eh? These days we'd probably keep our ex-nearest and ex-dearest in the deep-freeze and make sure we always pay the electricity bill. In ancient and extremely hot Egypt, however, they wrapped their kings' bodies up tightly (mummification) as this way, if done properly, they'd last for ever.

How to Mummify Your Best Friend in 10 Easy Stages

 1. Take one freshly dead best friend.

2. Wash him down with natron  (a natural washing soda).

 3. Pulp his brain (if he has one) and pull it through his nose with a hook.

4. Remove innards and  place in alabaster pots.

 5. Wrap heart and place back in body.

6. Replace any missing limbs with wooden ones.

7. Stuff rest of body with linen, sand, sawdust 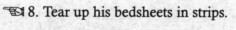 and aromatic spices to taste. As human bodies are 75% water (or in their case beer) this avoids shrinkage.

8. Tear up his bedsheets in strips.

9. Soak strips in gum and wrap 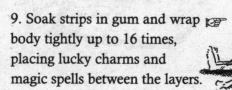 body tightly up to 16 times, placing lucky charms and magic spells between the layers.

10. Paint face on finished mummy (so that you can remember who he was) and insert artificial eyes.

11. Return to family.

PS. I'm not sure, but I *think* you can mummify ladies just as well (called daddies?).

Where to Put Them?

When it comes to burial we post-moderns usually dig a relatively small hole (for a relatively small relative) and are done with it – but not those ancient Egyptians. The posh ones went in for magnificent tombs in which their dead could rest in great luxury. Best of all were the ones topped with pyramids – huge pointy mountains of stone blocks, taller than any other buildings in the world. The pyramid at Giza remained the tallest structure in the world until the Eiffel tower was built in 1889.

Useless Fact No. 380*

The great pyramid of Cheops contained enough stone to build a three metre wall around France, and many wish that they'd done just that (sorry, France).

*I'm afraid the other 379 were too useless to put in. Ed

How to Build a King-Size Pyramid (just like the one at Giza).

1. Ring Imhotep (the top pyramid builder) for advice*.

2. Gather your workforce. This was easy as there were thousands of pleasant peasant farmers lounging around during the wet season (3 months) waiting for the floods to go down.

3. Get some stone blocks (2.6 million or so) each weighing between 2.5 and 15 tons. You'll also need rollers, ropes, sledges, levers, ramps and lubricating oil (failing that, a lorry or a crane).

4. Make a base of about 31 acres.

5. Pile up layers (about 200) making each one a few blocks smaller than the one below and making sure that there is no more than one thousandth of a centimetre gap between them (demanding or what?). Remember to stop when you get to just one block on the top.

6. Cover in white, polished limestone to make shiny.

7. Dig miles of passages and lots of dummy chambers in and around the star burial chamber to store all the boss's furniture and also to fool robbers.

8. Insert one dead king and lots of dead servants to look after him. If a bit squeamish about murdering the servants, use models (Naomi Campbell?).

9. Seal up.

10. If you have any blocks left over – tough: you're obviously not as fantastically good at geometry as those old Egyptians were.

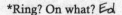

*Ring? On what? Ed

A Few Fascinating Facts about Pyramids and Tombs

⚠ Tombs often got raided by the deceased person's enemies, who'd nick the stiff and destroy the name and portrait carved on the door, so preventing his (or her, I suppose) passage to the next world (the gods, you see, wouldn't know who they were).

Useless Fact No. 387

Some Pharaohs had loos in their pyramids (in case they were caught short in the long afterlife).

⚠ The pyramids are all close to the Nile where the ships could unload (you try carrying 2.6 million tons of stone across a desert).

⚠ Tourists have been visiting (and robbing) the tombs ever since the ancient Greeks arrived.

⚠ The most untouched tomb ever found contained the 3000-year-old body of 15-year-old junior Pharaoh Tutankhamun. There is said to be a curse on anyone who visits it (but not, I hope, anyone who writes about it*). It's a long and utterly fascinating story, but I haven't got time to go into it now. Sorry.

*And not, I hope, anyone who reads about it! Ed

Chapter 10

BACK TO SCHOOL

If you are one of my female readers, I'm terribly sorry, but it might be just as well to ignore this chapter. Young ladies in ancient Egypt were not deemed worthy of education, which seems a trifle unfair in these liberated days. All they were expected to do was look pretty, dance nicely and, if they didn't have servants, cook and clean for the menfolk (so what's changed? I hear you cry). And if you want to get really mad – peasant women were worth less than cows. I did warn you, girls.

Your average Egyptian boy would have probably preferred it the other way round too. He'd had a great time as a little kid, larking about in the sunshine, fishing and swimming and generally avoiding being eaten by lions or crocodiles. But eventually Mater and Pater demanded he should attend the temple for a formal education (unless they were so blinking rich that they could have the teacher come round their house).

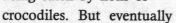

NOT INVENTED YET: Ed.

First of all young Tutt (for want of a better name) was taught to read and write. He'd sit cross-legged (or just plain cross) in the gloomy, silent temple, wooden writing palette in one hand and rush brush in the other, repeatedly scrubbing out what he'd done wrong and starting over.

tpygE tneicnA ni gnitirW

Egyptian writing was back to front (or right to left) and called Hieroglyphic. This was invented in 3000 BC and nobody really bothered to change it for 4000 years. It consisted of a lot of words and little pictures, so it took simply ages to get right. If, for instance, you decided to send a post-parchment to your granny thanking her for your birthday present, it could take until practically the next birthday to finish it.

Some bright spark, therefore, invented a quick version called *Hieratic,* and then some even brighter spark came up with *Demotic,* a super-duper, double-quick version which was a bit like our modern shorthand.

Oh Rosetta!

If a French army officer hadn't tripped over a small black tablet covered in funny writing, which came to be known as the Rosetta Stone, in 1799, we'd be none the wiser as to what the ancients were going on about. Mind you, I don't suppose the Egyptians would have cared. They certainly didn't give a fig about foreigners (or even give a fig *to* foreigners), so why should they bother about whether they could read their writing? Figs, it must be noted, grew plentifully throughout the Upper and Lower Egypt and were a staple par . . . *

. . . Ah yes, two of these pieces of writing were in Egyptian (hieroglyphic and demonic) and one was Greek. It took until 1822 for a jolly clever French homme called Champollion to

*Please get on with it. Ed

work out that the texts were connected. Luckily he understood the Greek one, so was able to crack the code. Simple eh?

Unfortunately not. Life's never that easy (even if you're dead clever). The ancient scribes, bless 'em, had apparently gone one stage further to confuse future Egyptologists, by leaving out all the vowel sounds (probably so that they could get home earlier). So instead of writing, 'Sorry dear, I'll be late for supper' they'd put 'Srry dr, b lt fr sppr.'

Anyway, the poor Egyptian boys would be forced (on pain of severe bottom lashing) to copy out scroll after scroll of never-ending , dead boring, ancient legends. Who says the girls got the worst deal?

Adding and Taking Away

Oddly enough Arithmetic was easier. This might well have been because their ancestors hadn't really got Multiplication or Division together, let alone Fractions or Algebra. (The world had to wait for the Arabs to work those out.) They were, however, astonishingly good at Geometry (particularly triangles) which became rather helpful when building pyramids.

Basically, it could be said that the Egyptians only developed the sums they needed on a day-to-day basis (which is about as far as I got). They didn't even have to worry about money as it hadn't been invented yet, so they used either barter or gold- and metal-dust (or ugly wives). They weren't 'in the money', so to speak, until the end of the Late Period. By the end of his education, therefore, a bright Egyptian boy could expect to read and write, add and subtract and would have a passing knowledge of all the ancient texts. He'd also be fair to middling at drawing and painting.

Chapter 11

FUN AND GAMES

There wasn't much to do fun-wise in the desert regions of Egypt apart from sunbathing and building sandcastles. But in the Valley and the Delta it was a very different story. Unlike temperate climates (what we live in) where we never know what the weather's going to be like from one minute to the next, they could guarantee bright sunlight (with no ozone holes) and warm evenings for most of the year. Quite a lot of their sports and leisure activities, therefore, were likely to be outdoors.

Cart Racing

If you were rich, the favourite sport amongst the young men was chariot racing. The invention of the wheel speeded this activity up considerably (before that chariot racing could be a bit of a drag – ha-ha!*).

When not chariot racing they got their bows and arrows out and shot at targets while galloping on horseback. Wrestling was also big in ancient Egypt and the kings used to enjoy watching their best soldiers practising on their slaves.

Huntin', Shootin' and Fishin'

When bored with simply racing, young men would get their chariots out and their dogs (a bit like greyhounds) to hunt lions which were simply everywhere in ancient times. The less energetic would stand on the river banks and chuck spears at

*Haven't we seen that joke before? Ed

crocs and hippos. And don't go thinking the Aborigines had cornered the market in the boomerang. Very early paintings show wily Egyptians throwing curved sticks at flights of ducks. They probably didn't hit any, but at least they tried, even taking their retriever-cats (really) with them, just in case.

DEAD
DUCK

And the Kids

Being young must have been a bit of a laugh. For a start they had brilliant pets like parrots, monkeys and ponies, as well as prototype cats and dogs. Anything smaller they usually ate (hamster-burgers and rat-atouille). After tea they'd gaze wistfully at the corner where the telly would be if it had been invented, and then go out to play ball games, leapfrog, whip and top and an antique version of hopscotch. Dolls for the girls were like miniature adults with articulated limbs – kind of ancient Barbies and Kens (Cleos and Tutts?).

Grown-Up Time

After reading the evening papyrus, while mum was organizing the washing-up, dad would have a couple of mates round, break out the beer and play draughts. They also had an early version of serpents and ladders, without the ladders (which, if you think about it, sounds a bit hopeless). If they were lucky, the better-looking slave girls would come out and dance for them topless (and often bottomless), save for the odd bead collar or belt which they'd jiggle about (amongst other things) to the satisfaction of all.*

Music was everywhere: in the streets, at banquets and even in the front room. Their instruments were the ancient relatives of the ones we use today. They had trumpets, harps, guitars, flutes and long double horns that sounded like mournful cows with gut-ache. Best of all was the rhythm section; they loved bashing and tapping anything that came to hand (particularly slaves). Weirdest of all was the *sistrum,* a small instrument with a bull's head on top. Metal wires hung with little discs were strung between the horns and when plucked sounded . . . absolutely dreadful (but apparently had a calming effect on evil spirits and women in labour). Maybe they should be used in haunted houses (and maternity wings).

The Downside of Having a Good Time in Ancient Egypt
1. No telly.

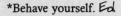

*Behave yourself. Ed

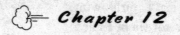

Chapter 12

OLD ART IN
NEW EGYPT

Before we get onto the good stuff of the Pharaoh period, art in Egypt looked much the same as the cave paintings that were being daubed on walls throughout the rest of the world: stylized men and animals with no clothes on*; primitive boats and frying – sorry – flying fish. In those days there were no artists as such, as the work was being carried out by the same chaps who'd been out doing a hard day's hunting and gathering.

The first professional artists came along much later when the great Egyptian civilization was revved-up and running. Unlike these days, when artists are regarded as something special (though heaven knows why), the people who recorded everyday life in their pictures were treated just the same as everyone else. They didn't bother to sign their work (maybe 'cos nobody really cared who'd done it).

. . . art in Heaven
Art in ancient Egypt served one main purpose – and it wasn't just as something pretty to hang over the mantelpiece (which they didn't have anyway). It was to show off the people who were being painted (and who paid the bill), their lives and their surroundings in the most perfect way possible – because that was the way that they wanted to continue into the afterlife (fair

*Animals don't wear clothes. Ed

enough?). Pictures, you see, became religious and sacred before the paint was even dry. So this is why you don't tend to get a lot of too tall, too short, too old, too ugly, too sick or too poor folk hanging around in Egyptian art.

Confusion Reigns

Egyptian artists, unfortunately, became a little mixed up when trying to draw these 'perfect' people. They couldn't quite get their heads round the difference between the head-on and side-on view. Next time you're in an Egyptian tomb*, look at any old painting and you'll see what I'm getting at. The head is painted in profile, but the eye appears sort of front-on. The shoulders and upper body are seen from the front, but the hips and legs from the side. Worse than that, they drew both the feet exactly the same (with the big toes on the same side).

Now, either Egyptians had developed a weird way of standing and *did* actually have two left feet (easier for shoemakers methinks), or the artists had lost the plot somewhere. It all comes down to perspective as a method of illustrating depth. Sadly this was not used until those clever-dick Greeks invented it. This meant that everything from landscapes to shopping centres were painted in the same flat, side-on method – a bit like a map.

* Oh! Regularly! Ed

Therefore . . .

If they wanted to show 253 soldiers, 5 princesses, 11 cows (or a partridge in a pear tree) it never occurred to them to put one behind another to save space, like in real life. They simply painted them in rows. Also, if one person was more important than another, they'd paint him bigger (crikey, I dread to think how big they'd paint me). It was logical and daft at the same time. Mind you, who's complaining? This style was to become really useful as historical documentation: if it hadn't been for these paintings, we'd know practically nothing about their lifestyles (and I wouldn't have been able to write this book*).

THAT'S YOU DOWN THERE

. . . and Sculpture

Carving and chipping images out of wood and stone was much more of a team effort. If it was to be stone, you'd start with the

*Arguably, no great loss. Ed

stone-mason who could split the rocks with amazing precision. He'd then take the rough block to the sculptor or, if it was too big, make the sculptor come to the block. If it was quite big, but not too big, they'd meet halfway. If it was slightly on the big side, but not . . .*

Anyway, wherever the blinking block ended up, the sculptor would chip and chop it into a recognizable 'thing'. Along comes the metal worker who adds eyes, bows and arrows etc. Off it then goes to the painter who decorates it to make it as lifelike as possible. Each of these blokes was respected as a craftsman in his own right, but nothing more. They certainly weren't given a private-view party with loads of bubbly and sausages on sticks.

I don't know about you, but if I'd slaved for months or even years over a piece of work, I'd have been pretty miffed to see it shut up in some dusty tomb, never to see the light of day.

What's Left?

When viewing Egyptian art it's important to remember that, because of the damage of time, vandals and the wicked work of the pyramid pirates, we only see the weeniest fraction (one ten-thousandth) of the amazing stuff produced. Mind you, if we didn't have that one ten-thousandth, this book would have been even shorter.

*Get on with it. Ed

Chapter 13

KEEPING IT CLEAN

You might be tempted, if you ever walked down main street Cairo, to think that the ancient Egyptians must have been a pretty filthy, smelly lot. Having no chimneys in their houses, no proper loos, nowhere to put rubbish (apart from the Nile) and terrible overcrowding certainly didn't help. Nor did the fact that it was usually hot enough to cook a sweaty cat (and its resident fleas).

But you'd be very wrong. The ancient Egyptians were clean to the point of squeakiness. Not only did they keep their houses spotless, but also their bodies. As usual the poor got the rotten end of the deal. They had to take their scratchy soapy paste (made from ashes and salts of natron), and usually their clothes down to the river where they'd splash about in the none-too-clean shallows.

The rich sent theirs to the laundry and had bathrooms and even showers (well, if you call a servant tipping water over you a shower). Having no indoor water supply meant that water had to dragged in by the slaves from the nearest well. After drying themselves off, the bathers would smother themselves in scented oils, as some sort of protection from the sun and sand. Then it was Make-Up Time.

The 8-Step Way to Achieve the Cleopatra Look

1. Apply mud pack made from powdered alum (or just splosh on some wrinkle and spot removing lotion – even ancients had zits).

2. Soak for an hour in a bath of warm asses' milk (if a little short on asses, ask milko to deliver 75 extra pints).

3. If not wearing a wig today, plump up hair to desired effect and add beads and jewels to taste.

4. Remove any surplus facial hairs (beards, moustaches, etc.) with silver tweezers or pumice stone.

5. Draw a thick almond-shaped ring round each eye with a little brush and a bottle of kohl (made from malachite).

6. Get out your red ochre powder and rub gently on lips and cheeks (of face!).

7. Take some hair henna to stain finger and toe nails, and (most oddly) the palms of hands and soles of feet.

8. Sprinkle with one of your many perfumes from your large collection of exquisite and priceless hand-crafted alabaster perfume jars.

This procedure, I'm told, also works for girls.

At the Doctor's

Going to an Egyptian doctor was a hit and miss affair. They were OK at the things you could actually see – broken bones, cuts and grazes, pulling out teeth and babies, but the rest was a dangerous cocktail of magic, folklore and dodgy guesswork. You'd have thought all that cutting up and embalming people would have taught them something about what goes on inside their personal bodies. 'Fraid not.

58

Despite whipping stiffs' innards out on a regular basis, they regarded close examination of said innards for medical reasons a trifle intrusive and rather tacky. Instead they went straight to the medicine cupboard. If a

SEEN ANYTHING YOU RECOGNISE?

certain potion didn't work – tough – it was probably due to the wrong spell or, more probably, the wrong god.

Useless Fact No. 391

To get rid of mice, they smothered the house in fat made from boiled-up cats. (Presumably, to get rid of cats they smothered the house with fat from boiled-up dogs).

The Downside of Egyptian Hygiene and Medicine

⚠ Lavs looked all right from the outside, with nice seats made of wood or marble, but underneath them were the equivalent of cat-litter trays containing ordinary sand.

⚠ No loo paper.

⚠ Feeling a little poorly? If the doctor couldn't actually *see* the problem – forget it – or start praying (make sure it's to the right god).

⚠ To cure blindness, take a pig's eye, mix it together with honey and red ochre and – wait for it – pour it in the poor patient's ears. (Blimey, I reckon the patient would end up blind *and* deaf!)

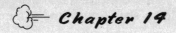

Chapter 14

GODS-A-PLENTY

Trying to sort out the complexities of Egyptian religion is a bit like attempting to explain American football to a three-year-old, until Christianity put a stop to it all anyway (Egyptian religion – not American football). Basically it was all about lots and lots of different gods who fought for power and rank among their Ancient Egyptian public.

At the top of the league they had the sun, the life giver, the starter of it all. The sun was also a god (naturally) and went under a couple of nom de plumes – Ra and Atum. Atum came to earth as Pharaoh, and rather cleverly reproduced himself (ask your teacher how – *I'm* not saying!) as Tefnut (*not* Tuffnut) and Shu. His lady was a goddess called Iusaas. Shu's grandson Geb (who was the earth) met a goddess called Nut (whom I personally would have avoided like the plague) who was the sky, and they produced four nippers. Two of these were little godlets called Osiris and Seth who married Isis and Nephthys. Still with me?

Other Gods of Interest

⚠ Heh and Hehet – gods of eternity.

⚠ Quite difficult to see, Tenem and Tenemet – god and goddess of twilight.

⚠ Even more difficult to see, Kek and Keket – god and goddess of darkness.

△ Totally impossible to see, Amun and Amunet, god and goddess of hiddenness.

△ Min, always shown with arm holding whip and crown with two plumes, represented mummies. He's usually shown holding something else as well.*

△ Ram-headed Khumn, whose job was to make the earth fertile, and was married to goddess Satet. He made the earth on his potter's wheel (just think, it could have looked like a teapot).

△ Ptar, patron of the arts and crafts, and his missus Sekhmet (a real babe, if you're into lion-headed women).

△ Hathor, daughter of Ra, who was asked to destroy mankind because of their disrespect. Success rate: zero.

△ Mut, goddess of motherhood (shouldn't that be mutherhood?).

△ Bastet (no jokes please), the goddess of the ointment jar (sticky position).

△ Thoth, god of knowledge (and lispers), who went around as a baboon (clever baboons? I think not). He was part-time god of the moon as well.

△ The god of the river was called Haapi. The ancient Egyptians, to whom the Nile meant everything, went to great lengths to keep Haapi happy.**

△ By far the most important and most talked-about gods were Horus and the Osiris, who popped up everywhere. Horus had the head of a falcon and represented kingship, while Osiris was god of the dead and represented the underworld.

*But we won't go into that, will we? Ed
**Please! Ed

Brotherly Love (a short story)

God Osiris never got on with brother god Seth (which might have something to do with Seth's weasely snout, forked tail, tall, straight ears and generally unpleasant manner). This was proved when Seth, jealous of his brother's position as top king, invited him to a slap-up dinner and presented the latest thing in coffins, the sort that absolutely anyone who was anyone would have loved to be seen dead in. Seth told them that the person who fitted it best could have it (shades of Cinderella?). Osiris jumped in and was delighted with the snug fit. Seth rather unkindly slammed shut the lid and promptly threw it (plus brother) in the Nile (a fine way to treat a dinner guest). Isis, who was both Osiris's wife *and* sister (shock, horror!!)

FITS YOU A TREAT

went out to find him. She finally tracked him down, well dead, inside the trunk of a living tree, up Lebanon way, which you must admit was pretty fair detective work. Seth, majorly miffed, cut his dead brother into tiny pieces and chucked them back in the river (it never rains but it pours). Isis, with the help of Seth's wife (nice of her), collected all of the pieces – which had floated far and wide throughout Lower Egypt. She magically put *all* the pieces back so well that she and the reconstituted Osiris conceived a son. Osiris had, by this time, had quite enough (can you blame him) and descended to work on the underground*. Their

I THINK I CAN GUESS WHERE THIS LAST BIT GOES

lad Horus hid with his mum in the Delta marshes until he was a bigger god. Then he, harpoon in hand, went after the dreadful Seth, who promptly turned into a hippopotamus (as one does). They remained bitter enemies until eventually Horus was given the settled land of Egypt to rule over and Seth, as a bit of a booby prize, the desert.

*Shouldn't that be 'underworld'? Ed

All in One

Just to muck things up completely, each successive Pharaoh had to combine the two gods Horus and Seth within himself (hence the double crown). I don't know about you but, in the light of the above, that would have sent the likes of me out to see a shrink forthwith.

Just to make sure you've been paying attention, here's a test.

△ Who were Atum's children?

△ Who was Geb's grandson?

△ Who did Osiris marry?

△ What sort of head did Horus wear?

△ Who won the Cup Final in 1971?

Downsides of Being a God

1. All the other gods were always trying to do you down – or worse.

2. You sometimes found yourself having to double as a hat or a chair.

☁ TIME'S UP

I'm the first to admit that as histories of Ancient Egypt go, mine has been a little on the brief side. Having said that, if you know a bit more than you knew before, and you haven't found this vast work too strenuous, then what more do you expect for the price of a cheeseburger (without fries)?

If I've whetted your appetite for more about Egypt, then might I suggest that you drag yourself along to the library and wade through all the trillions of words already written on the subject.

On the other hand, if, like me, you feel that you now know all you need to know, why not quit while you're winning, and try one of the other books in this series.

Don't be in too much of a hurry, however, as I might not have written 'em yet.